Imprint:

Copyright © 2018 GRIN Verlag
Print and binding: Books on Demand GmbH, Norderstedt Germany
ISBN: 9783668933446

This book at GRIN:

https://www.grin.com/document/464340

Wassim Al Chamaa

MATLAB Implementation of the Steganographic Algorithm F5

Matlab Codes for F5 Algorithm

GRIN Verlag

GRIN - Your knowledge has value

Since its foundation in 1998, GRIN has specialized in publishing academic texts by students, college teachers and other academics as e-book and printed book. The website www.grin.com is an ideal platform for presenting term papers, final papers, scientific essays, dissertations and specialist books.

Visit us on the internet:

http://www.grin.com/

http://www.facebook.com/grincom

http://www.twitter.com/grin_com

MATLAB Implementation of the Steganographic Algorithm F5

By

Wassim Al Chamaa

TABLE OF CONTENTS

ABSTRACT

The F5 algorithm proposed by Westfeld is still one of the most known algorithms in the field of DCT-based steganography. It can make a JPEG image a container of a secret message, where no one knows the presence of the message except the sender and the intended receiver. In this programming work, we show how to realize the F5 algorithm via Matlab. We will present the block diagrams of embedding and extracting processes and the entire Matlab codes of the F5 algorithm.

LIST OF FIGURES

4

1. Introduction to JPEG-based Steganography

Steganography is a data hiding technique that has been used in the applications of information protection. It transmits a secret message by hiding it into a cover object in order to create a hidden way of communication. Steganography has the same goal as cryptography since they aim to protect sensitive information. But they differ in the way of working; Cryptography converts the plain message into an unreadable encrypted message where the presence of the cryptography is not concealed, while steganography smuggles the message by embedding it into an innocent-looking object and thus creating an invisible communication channel.

The techniques of steganography have been developed in the field of digital objects such as JPEG images, where we can make the JPEG image a container for a secret message by embedding the message Bits within it. The JPEG image will represent a hidden communication channel, where no one knows what it contains except the sender and intended receiver. Many JPEG-based steganographic methods have been invented in the DCT domain, including the F5 algorithm developed by Westfeld [1]. The F5 algorithm was born in 2001 and is still one of the more known methods.

2. F5 Steganographic Method

Many of the DCT-based methods are based on the idea of a hash function. The function hashes a specific number (n) of quantized DCT coefficients (qDCT) to produce a specific number (k) of Bits. When the sender wants to embed a secret (k) Bits message, the (n) qDCT coefficients should be modified accordingly. Thus, when the receiver hashes the modified (n) qDCT coefficients, the hidden message is then obtained. The modifications are always constrained by requirements and rules depending on the considered algorithm.

The F5 algorithm was proposed by Westfeld [1]. It is based on the idea of the matrix encoding (dmax, n, k) with dmax=1, where its goal is to minimize the number of changes made to the qDCT coefficients. The F5 algorithm takes (n) qDCT coefficients and hashes them to (k) Bits using a Xor-based hash function. When the sender needs a modification to embed the secret message, only one coefficient is changed since the resulting (n) qDCT coefficients should not have a hamming distance of more than dmax=1 from the original (n) qDCT coefficients. The (k) and (n) are calculated based on the original image capacity as well as the message length.

3. Matlab Implementation of F5 Algorithm
3.1 Huffman Coding and Decoding

The DCT-based steganographic methods are based on the idea of modifying the qDCT coefficients in such a way allowing to embed a stream of Bits. Thus, we need to have the ability to access the qDCT coefficients of a given JPEG file. The Matlab's built-in functions used to handle digital images provide only basic conversion between the given JPEG file and image pixels. They don't give any access to the qDCT coefficients. In order to overcome this issue, we use a dedicated Matlab JPEG Toolbox developed by Sallee [2]. The used JPEG Toolbox contains special functions allowing to access and manipulate the qDCT coefficients of a given JPEG file.

The main two functions in the Sallee's package "jpeg_read" and "jpeg_write" perform the steps of the lossless compression applied to the qDCT coefficients including Huffman coding and decoding. Thus, they provide more functionality, since they give the ability to gain direct access to all the structural elements of a JPEG file from Matlab, including the matrices of qDCT coefficients and the quantization tables.

3.2 Implementation of F5 Embedding Process
3.2.1 Steps of F5 Embedding Process

In this section, we present a block diagram showing the implementation steps of the F5 algorithm on the sender side of the connection, where we hide the message file into a given JPEG image.

At first, the "jpeg_read" function reads the given JPEG file and performs the entropy decoding. The "jpeg_read" function gives a Matlab structure containing the qDCT coefficients matrices, quantization tables, and other information. Only the qDCT coefficients matrix of Y component is used to embed the secret message because of its large size compared to those of the other two components.

Before running the F5 embedding process, we should have two tasks completed:
1. We define the matrix encoding ME by calculating the size of the message file and the number of Non-zero coefficients in the resulting Y matrix. The ME calculator gives the initial value of the matrix encoding that we should use in the embedding process.
2. Typically, the embedding process should be protected and connected with a secret key. Thus, we should use a key-based permutation generator. The generated permutation is applied to the qDCT coefficients matrix of Y component before running the F5_ME embedding process.

During the running of the F5 embedding process, we take into consideration the shrinkage of Non-zero qDCT coefficients, thus a shrinkage tester is always running. The tester aims to detect the occurrence of the shrinkage during the process, so the shrinking coefficient will be replaced by another one. In addition, the tester aims to ensure that the message file was embedded entirely according to the used ME, otherwise, the ME will be recalculated and the embedding process will be repeated according to the new ME.

In the end, the resulting matrix is inversely permuted in order to get back the original order of the Y matrix of qDCT coefficients. The resulting qDCT coefficients matrix of Y component will then be in the same order as the original one, but with some modifications caused by the embedding process of the F5 algorithm. At this point, we write the resulting matrix to the Matlab JPEG structure and then use the "jpeg_write" function to perform the entropy coding in order to produce the Stego JPEG file that contains the secret message file. A block diagram of the F5 embedding process is presented in Figure 1.

6

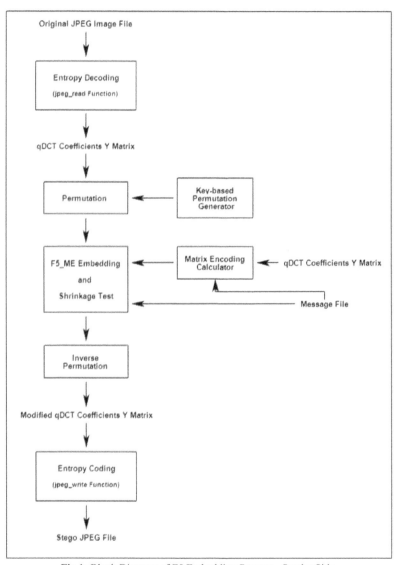

Fig 1: Block Diagram of F5 Embedding Process - Sender Side.

7

3.2.2 Main Script and Called Functions

Main Script	Called Functions	m Files
	Msgsize Function	Msgsize.m
	Qdct2Img Function	Qdct2Img.m
	MediCap Function	MediCap.m
	MatEncod Function	MatEncod.m
F5Embed Main Script - F5Embed.m	GetkBits Function	GetkBits.m
	DoEmbed Function	DoEmbed.m
	DoStego Function	DoStego.m
	F5Hash Function	F5Hash.m
	DoChange Function	DoChange.m
	HistPlot Function	HistPlot.m

3.2.3 Matlab Codes of F5 Embedding Process

In this section, we present the entire Matlab codes, main script and called functions, that realize the embedding process of a secret message file whatever its extension.

3.2.3.1 F5Embed Matlab Main Script

```
clear all; close all; clc;
OriginalImg='CoverImage.JPG';        % Original image file - Cover Image.
Messagefile='Message.txt';           % Secret Message file, whatever the extension.
SteganoImg='StegoImage.JPG';         % Resulting image file - Stego Image.
Msgbits=Msgsize(Messagefile);
JPG=jpeg_read(OriginalImg);          % Reading original image file / Huffman decoding.
mat1=JPG.coef_arrays{1};             % Y component matrix
Qtb1=JPG.quant_tables{JPG.comp_info(1).quant_tbl_no};
img1= Qdct2Img(mat1,Qtb1);
figure(1);
imshow(img1);                        % showing Y component of the Original image.
Cap=MediCap(mat1);                   % Calculating Nonzero coefficients.
siz=size(mat1);
Rw=siz(1);            % rows      : Height.
Cl=siz(2);           % columms : Width.
CoefNb=Cl*Rw;
TmpBuff=zeros(1,CoefNb);   % Temporary Buffer.
RltBuff=zeros(1,CoefNb);    % Resulting Buffer.
%
indx=0;
for xx=1:Rw
  for yy=1:Cl
    indx=indx+1;
    TmpBuff(indx)=mat1(xx,yy);
  end
end
% Now, we have (indx=CoefNb).
```

```
% ...................
% At this point, a permutation should be applied to the Temporary Buffer : TmpBuff
% ...................
Embrate= 100*(Msgbits/Cap);
Encod=MatEncod(Embrate);      % Calculating Matrix Encoding.
% ................... Main Processing LOOP ...................
WrkCn=0;        % Counter of work process
WrkDone=0;
while(WrkDone==0)     % Main Processing LOOP
  WrkCn=WrkCn+1;
  % Available codewords number (Cap/n).
  AvalCdWd=(Cap-mod(Cap,Encod(2)))/Encod(2);
  % Needed codewords number (Msgbits/k).
  NeedCdWd=(Msgbits-mod(Msgbits,Encod(3)))/Encod(3);
  % Stego Operation, We have :    AvalCdWd > NeedCdWd
  SecData=GetkBits(Messagefile,Encod(3));
  mBuff=zeros(1,1);
  ShkgCn=0;  % Shrinkage counter.
  cont=0;        % (n) nonzero counter.
  indx=1;
  ix=1;
  CdWd=1;      % Codeword index.
  while ((CdWd<=NeedCdWd) && (indx <= CoefNb))
          while ((cont<Encod(2)) && (indx <= CoefNb))
              if (TmpBuff(indx)==0)
                mBuff(ix)=TmpBuff(indx);
                indx=indx+1;
                ix=ix+1;
              elseif (TmpBuff(indx)~=0)
                mBuff(ix)=TmpBuff(indx);
                cont=cont+1;
                indx=indx+1;
                ix=ix+1;
              end
          end
      if(indx <= CoefNb)
          m=ix-1; % the buffered number.
          % Now, we have (cont=Encod(2)).
          MBuff_shk=DoEmbed(mBuff,m,Encod(2),SecData(CdWd));
          if (MBuff_shk{1,2}==0)     % No Shrinkage.
            OutBuffs{1,CdWd}=MBuff_shk{1,1};
            CdWd=CdWd+1;
            mBuff=zeros(1,1);
            cont=0;
            ix=1;
          elseif (MBuff_shk{1,2}==1) % Shrinkage.
            ShkgCn=ShkgCn+1;
            ShkPot=MBuff_shk{1,3};
            mBuff(ShkPot)=0;
            cont=cont-1;
          end
      end
  end
end
```

9

```
  if (indx > CoefNb)        % The case where (indx) exceeded (CoefNb)
     Embrate=100*(Encod(3)/Encod(2));
     Encod=MatEncod(Embrate);  % Recalculating Encod
     WrkDone=0;                 % The work is NOT done
  end
  if (CdWd > NeedCdWd) % The case where the work is done
     WrkDone=1;
  end
end        % End of Main Processing LOOP
% ..............................................................
% ...............End of Main Processing LOOP..................
% ..............................................................
ChgMax=ShkgCn+NeedCdWd; % Maximum number of changes.
BffLmt=indx-1;                % Reached limit in TmpBuff.
% End of Stego Operation
%
% Constructing Resulting Buffer : RltBuff
Concat=[OutBuffs{1,1} OutBuffs{1,2}];
for i=3:NeedCdWd  % Concatenation.
  Concat=[Concat OutBuffs{1,i}];
end
Sz=size(Concat);
for i=1:Sz(2)
  RltBuff(i)=Concat(i);
end
for i=Sz(2)+1:CoefNb
  RltBuff(i)=TmpBuff(i);
end
% ....................
% At this point, In case we used Permutation, The inverse Permutation
% should be applied to the Resulting Buffer : RltBuff
% ....................
% Histogram of resulting Buffer.
figure(2);
HH=HistPlot(RltBuff,25,0,0);
% Constructing New Coefficients Matrix.
siz=size(mat1);
Rw=siz(1);     % rows    : Height.
Cl=siz(2);     % columms : Width.
Nmat1=zeros(Rw,Cl);
inx=0;
for xx=1:Rw
  for yy=1:Cl
    inx=inx+1;
    Nmat1(xx,yy)=RltBuff(inx);
  end
end
% Now, we have (inx=CoefNb).
%
% Stego image Reconstruction
JPG.coef_arrays{1}=Nmat1;         % New Coefficients Matrix (Y component).
jpeg_write(JPG,SteganoImg);
%
```

```matlab
% showing the Stego image (Y component).
JPG=jpeg_read(SteganoImg);
mat1=JPG.coef_arrays{1};
Qtb1=JPG.quant_tables{JPG.comp_info(1).quant_tbl_no};
img2= Qdct2Img(mat1,Qtb1);
figure(3);
imshow(img2);
%
```

3.2.3.2 Msgsize Matlab Function

```matlab
function bitSize=Msgsize(msgfile)
%
fileObj = memmapfile(msgfile);
siz = size(fileObj.data);
FileSiz=siz(1);              % File Size in Bytes.
bitSize= FileSiz*8;         % File Size in Bits.
%
```

3.2.3.3 Qdct2Img Matlab Function

```matlab
function img_mat= Qdct2Img(qdct_mat,Qtbl)
% This function computes the Image
% matrix of the considered component.
demat=dequantize(qdct_mat,Qtbl);
img_mat0=ibdct(demat)+128;
img_mat=uint8(img_mat0);
%
```

3.2.3.4 MediCap Matlab Function

```matlab
function  Cap=MediCap(mat)
% mat : Y component matrix.
siz=size(mat);
Rw=siz(1);      % rows : Height.
Cl=siz(2);       % columms : Width.
% Calculating the number of
% Nonzero coefficients.
cout=0;
for xx=1:Rw
  for yy=1:Cl
    if (mat(xx,yy)~=0)
     cout=cout+1;
    end
  end
end
Cap=cout;
%
```

3.2.3.5 MatEncod Matlab Function

```
function Encod=MatEncod(Embrate)
% Calculating the matrix encoding
Encod=[1 1 1];
k=0;
Diff=1;
while (Diff>0)
  k=k+1;
  R=100*(k /((2^k)-1));
  Diff=R-Embrate;
end
k=k-1;
n=(2^k)-1;
Encod(2)=n;
Encod(3)=k;
%
```

3.2.3.6 GetkBits Matlab Function

```
function  SecData=GetkBits(msgfile,k)
% Distribute the information to be hidden on a matrix
% Creating a matrix (SecData) including the Bits stream
% of the secret message file according to (k) value.
% msgfile : File name String.
%    k    : Embeded data size.
Frmt=['ubit' int2str(k)];
Msgbits=Msgsize(msgfile);
Nb=(Msgbits-mod(Msgbits,k))/k;
SecData=zeros(1,Nb);
fid=fopen(msgfile,'r');
for idx=1:Nb
  SecData(idx)= fread(fid,1,Frmt);
end
fclose(fid);
%
```

3.2.3.7 DoEmbed Matlab Function

```
function  MBuff_shk=DoEmbed(mBuff,m,n,DesiredVal)
% mBuff has the size (m) and contains (m) qDCT coefficients.
% mBuff contains (n) Nonzero qDCT coefficients.
% m >= n
% m : loop-changeable value.
% n : the encoding value, Matrix Encoding =(1,n,k).
% DesiredVal : the desired value to be embedded.
% DesiredVal will be within [0,1,..,n], k Bits.

  nBuff=zeros(1,n);
  j=0;
  for i=1:m
     if (mBuff(i)~=0)        % Nonzero values.
        j=j+1;
        nBuff(j)=mBuff(i);
        mBuff(i)=0.5;    % Marking the Nonzero value locations.
     end
  end
  % Now, we have (j=n).
  NBuff=zeros(1,n);
  % Appling F5 algorithm on nBuff.
  if(j==n)
     NBuff=DoStego(nBuff,n,DesiredVal);
  end
  % Reforming mBuff.
  % Shrinkage Testing in steganographed NBuff.
  Shk=0;     % Shrinkage Indicator.
  ShkPt=0;   % Shrinkage Position.
  j=0;
  for i=1:m
     if (mBuff(i)==0.5)
        j=j+1;
        mBuff(i)=NBuff(j);
        if (NBuff(j)==0)       % Shrinkage Test.
           Shk=1;                 % Shrinkage Indicator.
           ShkPt=i;               % Shrinkage Position.
        end
     end
  end
  % Now, we have (j=n).
  % mBuff has been modified/steganographed.
  %
  % Returning modified buffer.
  % and shrinkage indicator.
  MBuff=mBuff;
  MBuff_shk={MBuff,Shk,ShkPt};
  %
```

3.2.3.8 DoStego Matlab Function

```
function  stegoBuff=DoStego(Buff,n,DesiredVal)
% Buff contains (n) qDCTs coefficients.
% DesiredVal is the desired value to be embedded.
% DesiredVal will be within [0,1,..,n].
%
% Calculating the current Hash value.
CurrentVal=F5Hash(Buff,n);
% XORing desired and current values
% in order to find bit location (S) to modify.
S= bitxor(DesiredVal,CurrentVal);
% Applying the (d=1) modification :
% changing the buffer by One change
NewBuff=DoChange(Buff,S);
% Calculating the New Hash value.
NewVal=F5Hash(NewBuff,n);
% Comparing between
% New and Desired values
% Returning the stego Buffer.
if (NewVal==DesiredVal)          % Must be always true.
   stegoBuff=NewBuff;
 elseif (NewVal~=DesiredVal)
   stegoBuff=0;
  end
%
```

3.2.3.9 F5Hash Matlab Function

```
function Hash = F5Hash(Buff,n)
% F5 algorithm Hash function
% Buff contains (n) qDCTs coefficients.
ABuff= abs(Buff);       % (ai) Bits do not change.
B=ones(1,n);
a = bitand(ABuff,B);    % Extracting (ai) Bits values.
%%%
indx=zeros(1,n);
for i=1:n
 indx(i)=i;
end
%%%
idx=a.*indx;            % Multiplying element by element.
%%%
hsh=idx(1);
for i=2:n
 hsh= bitxor(hsh,idx(i));
end
Hash=hsh; % Resulting Hash Value.
%
```

3.2.3.10 DoChange Matlab Function

```matlab
function  NewBuff=DoChange(Buff,S)
% (S) points to the bit location that must be changed
% Treatement Only in case of (S>0), If (S=0) there is NO changment.
if  (S>0)
    if (Buff(S)> 0)          % Positive qDCT Value.
      Buff(S)= Buff(S)-1;
    elseif (Buff(S)< 0)      % Negative qDCT Value.
      Buff(S) = (-1)*(abs(Buff(S))-1);
    end
end
NewBuff=Buff;
%
```

3.2.3.11 HistPlot Matlab Function

```matlab
function HH=HistPlot(Vec,Rang,MaxCH,MaxCnt)

HH=zeros(1,3);
siz=size(Vec);
[n,xout]=hist(Vec,-Rang:Rang);
ToTNb=sum(n);
HH(1)=ToTNb;
XNb=(2*Rang)+1;
HH(2)=n(1)+n(XNb);
%%%
n(1)=0;
n(XNb)=0;
if (ToTNb==siz(2) && MaxCH==1)
    for i=1:XNb
      if(xout(i)==0)
        HH(3)=n(i);
        n(i)=MaxCnt;
      end
    end
end
bar(xout,n);
%
```

3.3 Implementation of F5 Extracting Process
3.3.1 Steps of F5 Extracting Process

In this section, we present a block diagram showing the implementation steps of the F5 algorithm on the receiver side of the connection, where we extract the hidden message file from the received Stego JPEG file.

At first, the Stego JPEG file is read (red) by the "jpeg_read" Matlab function which gives a Matlab structure containing the qDCT coefficients matrices. The qDCT coefficients matrix of **Y** component is then permuted using the same permutation generator and key which were used in the sender side. After permutation, we obtain the matrix in the same order that was used during the embedding process. The F5 algorithm will then hash the permuted matrix using the same matrix encoding ME that was used during the embedding process in order to get the hidden message File. A block diagram of the F5 extraction process is presented in Figure 2.

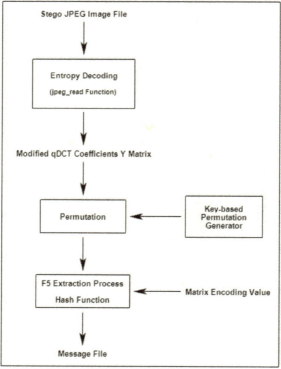

Fig 2: Block Diagram of F5 Extraction Process - Receiver Side.

3.3.2 Main Script and Called Functions

Main Script	Called Functions	m Files
F5Extract Main Script - F5Extract.m	MediCap Function DoExtract Function F5Hash Function	MediCap.m DoExtract.m F5Hash.m

3.3.3 Matlab Codes of F5 Extracting Process

In this section, we present the entire Matlab codes, main script and called functions, that realize the extracting process of the hidden message file. In order to extract the hidden file correctly, the Value of the Matrix Encoding, must be set as calculated in the embedding process.

3.3.3.1 F5Extract Matlab Main Script

```
clear all;close all; clc;
% In order to extract the hidden file correctly, the Value
% of Encod (Matrix Encoding) must be set as calculated in
% the embedding process : F5Embed.m .
% Used Matrix Encoding
Encod=[1 15 4];   % [1 7 3],[1,31,5],[1,63,6],[1,255,8];
%
StegoIm='StegoImage.JPG';      % Received Stego Image file.
Rcvmsg='Extracted.txt';        % Extracted Hidden Message file.
%
JPG=jpeg_read(StegoIm);
mat1=JPG.coef_arrays{1};
Cap=MediCap(mat1);
% Available codewords number (Cap/n).
AvalCdWd=(Cap-mod(Cap,Encod(2)))/Encod(2);
%
siz=size(mat1);
Rw=siz(1);        % rows    : Height.
Cl=siz(2);        % columms : Width.
CoefNb=Cl*Rw;
TmpBuff=zeros(1,CoefNb);
mBuff=zeros(1,1);
%
indx=0;
for xx=1:Rw
  for yy=1:Cl
    indx=indx+1;
    TmpBuff(indx)=mat1(xx,yy);
  end
end
```

```
% ...................
% At this point, we should apply the same permutation
% which was used in the embedding process to TmpBuff.
% ...................
cont=0;
CdWd=1;
indx=1;
ix=1;
ExVal=0;
while(CdWd<=AvalCdWd)                % Extraction LOOP
  while (cont<Encod(2))
       if (TmpBuff(indx)==0)
          mBuff(ix)=TmpBuff(indx);
          indx=indx+1;
          ix=ix+1;
       elseif (TmpBuff(indx)~=0)
          mBuff(ix)=TmpBuff(indx);
          cont=cont+1;
          indx=indx+1;
          ix=ix+1;
       end
  end
  m=ix-1;             % The bufferd number.
  ExVal=[ExVal DoExtract(mBuff,m,Encod(2))];
  CdWd=CdWd+1;
  mBuff=zeros(1,1);
  ix=1;
  cont=0;
end              % End of Extraction LOOP
% ................... % End of Extraction LOOP
% ...........................................................
% Writing extracted Bits stream to a file (secret message file).
k=Encod(3);
Frmt=['ubit' int2str(k)];
fid=fopen(Rcvmsg,'w');
for i=2:AvalCdWd+1
  count = fwrite(fid,ExVal(i),Frmt);  % Creating the output file.
end
fclose(fid);
%
```

3.3.3.2 MediCap Matlab Function

The function here is the same as in the section 3.2.3.4 .

3.3.3.3 DoExtract Matlab Function

```
function ExVal=DoExtract(mBuff,m,n)
%
nBuff=zeros(1,n);
j=0;
for i=1:m
   if (mBuff(i)~=0) % Nonzero values.
     j=j+1;
     nBuff(j)=mBuff(i);
   end
end
% Now, we have (j=n).
% Calculating the F5 Hash value.
ExVal=F5Hash(nBuff,n);
%
```

3.3.3.4 F5Hash Matlab Function

The function here is the same as in the section 3.2.3.9 .

4. Programming Notes:

1- In the DCT-based steganography, we need to have direct access to qDCT coefficients. The toolbox of Sallee made it easier for us to access and manipulate the qDCT coefficients where the main two functions of the package perform the standard steps of lossless compression including Huffman Coding and decoding. This toolbox provides complete control over all internal contents of the JPEG image file, thus it can be used in many applications especially in DCT-based steganography.

2- The embedding program starts from a given JPEG file stored on a digital storage unit and ends with an output Stego JPEG file to be stored or to be sent over the network. Therefore, Removing the codes of showing the images and histogram doesn't affect the main function of the program.

3- The secret message file can be any file of any kind and whatever its extension. The embedding and extracting programs deal with the message file as a series of Bits.

4- The shrinkage happening to qDCT coefficients during the embedding process is a subject to probability. It may affect the capacity of the image since it causes a decrease in the number of Non-zero qDCT coefficients. Therefore, the possibility of modifying the initially calculated value of ME during the embedding process and thus repeating the process should be taken into consideration.

5- In the presented program, the part related to the permutation is left blank where the programmer can add his own codes accordingly. The programmer can build a permutation generator based on a pseudo-random generator and connect it to a key.

References

[1]   A. Westfeld. "F5 — a steganographic algorithm — high capacity despite better steganalysis": Information Hiding, Fourth International Workshop, Lecture Notes in Computer Science vol. 2137, 289–302, 2001.

[2]   Phil Sallee. "Matlab JPEG Toolbox": Original package: jpegtbx_1.4, Sep 2003.

YOUR KNOWLEDGE HAS VALUE

- We will publish your bachelor's and
  master's thesis, essays and papers

- Your own eBook and book -
  sold worldwide in all relevant shops

- Earn money with each sale

Upload your text at www.GRIN.com
and publish for free